Table of Contents

No Tax, No Tea

Rally Mohawks! Bring out your axes.
And tell King George we'll pay no taxes.

*T*wo hundred men, their faces stained with soot, marched through the streets of Boston in the colony of Massachusetts. They were wrapped in Indian blankets and carried tomahawks and hatchets. It was six o'clock in the evening, December 16, 1773.

On reaching a wharf in Boston Harbor, they divided into three groups and boarded three ships. From the holds they hauled over 300 chests of tea, split them open and dumped them into the black water.

"And all the while we were surrounded by British ships. But no attempt was made to resist us," wrote one of the "Indians," sixty years later.

Though the first battles of the American Revolution were not fought until 1775, with the Boston Tea Party, the Revolution began.

The American Revolution did not start as a war for independence. During its first year, no Americans said they wanted to leave the British Empire. What they wanted was the restoration of their "Englishmen's Rights" within the Empire. These rights King George III and his government threatened.

George III became King of England in 1760 when he was an earnest, fussy, well-intentioned young man of twenty-three. One of his main goals was to be a strong ruler. His mother had urged, "George, be a king."

To George being a king meant interfering far more than most of his subjects liked with running the English government. With bribery and browbeating, he often succeeded in getting his own way. But not always. In the first ten years of his reign he tried and failed to choke freedom of speech and the press in England. In the next ten years, he tried to force "taxation without representation" on Americans. Again he failed and lost the American colonies in so doing.

When George became king, England was fighting a fierce war with France, the Seven Years War. This war came at the

King George III

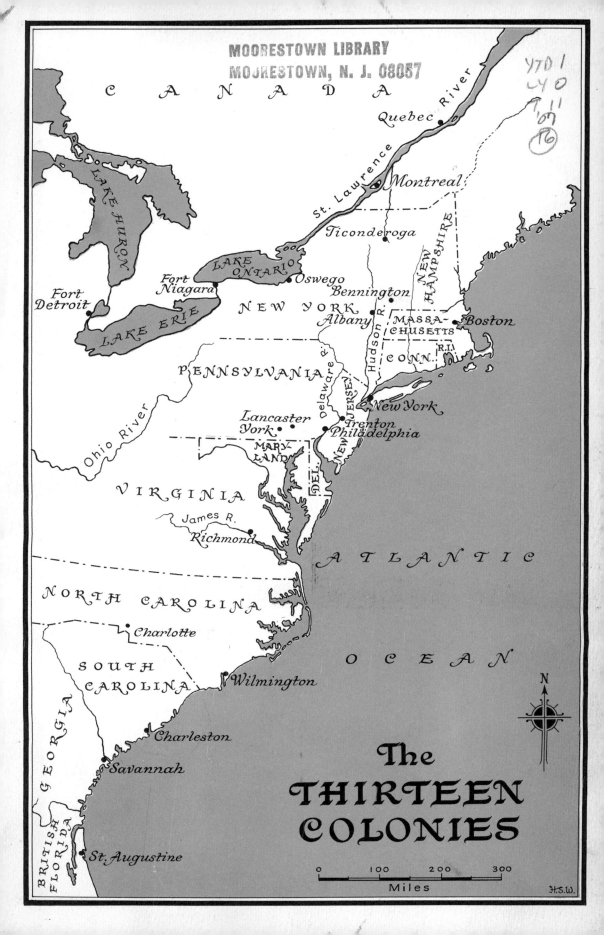

C A N A D A

Quebec

St. Lawrence River

Montreal

LAKE HURON

Ticonderoga

LAKE ONTARIO

Fort
Niagara

Oswego

Bennington

NEW YORK

Fort
Detroit

LAKE ERIE

NEW HAMPSHIRE

Albany

Hudson R.

MASSA-
CHUSETTS

Boston

CONN.

R.I.

PENNSYLVANIA

Ohio River

Delaware R.

NEW JERSEY

New York

Lancaster
York

Trenton
Philadelphia

MARY-
LAND

DEL.

V I R G I N I A

James R.

Richmond

A T L A N T I C

N O R T H   C A R O L I N A

Charlotte

O C E A N

SOUTH
CAROLINA

Wilmington

N

GEORGIA

Charleston

Savannah

The
THIRTEEN
COLONIES

BRITISH
FLORIDA

St. Augustine

0   100   200   300

Miles

H.S.W.

MOORESTOWN FREE LIBRARY
MOORESTOWN, N. J.

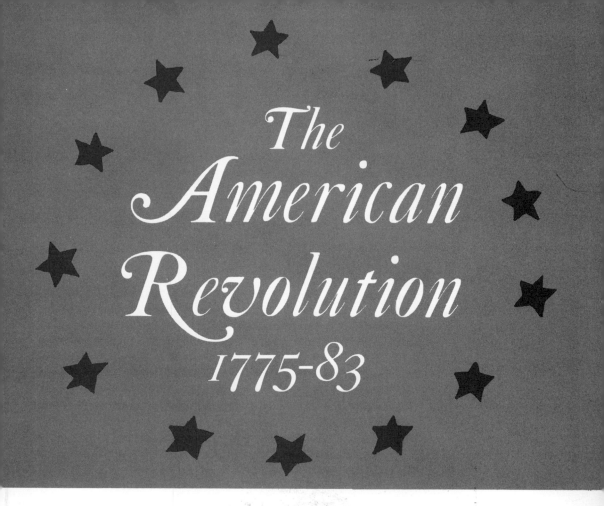

The American Revolution
1775-83

Contemporary drawings and engravings
Illustrations by H. Toothill and H. S. Whithorne

A British View

by Clorinda Clarke

McGRAW-HILL BOOK COMPANY
New York · St. Louis · Dallas · San Francisco

For my nephew, Frederic T. O'Hara

T
973.3
C

TO THE READER

This book was published in England in 1964 to tell English boys and girls about our Revolution. It is a small book and the Revolution was a very long war. It lasted eight years and is the longest war America ever fought. In this book I used British and redcoats for the King's Army; American and Rebels for the Revolutionary Army though both had other names.

Because I didn't have enough room to write about all the generals and battles, I tried to select the ones which had the greatest effect on the outcome of the Revolution—American independence. I have tried to give both sides of the story. Almost 200 years have passed since the Revolution and most American and British historians agree on why Americans fought and won their Revolution.

Clorinda Clarke

First Publication in the United States of America 1967
Copyright © Clorinda Clarke 1964
Library of Congress Catalog Number: 67-15851
First publication by Longmans, Green and Co Ltd, London, 1964

ACKNOWLEDGEMENTS

The maps are based on those in ATLAS OF AMERICAN HISTORY by James Truslow Adams. Copyright 1943 Charles Scribner's Sons

Pictures appearing on pages 11, 12, 13, 29, 41
Courtesy of the I. N. Phelps Stokes Collection of American Historical Prints, Prints Division, The New York Public Library.

Pictures on pages 25, 49
Courtesy of the Spencer Collection, The New York Public Library
Astor, Lenox and Tilden Foundations

end of a 70-year period of off-and-on fighting between England and France over Europe, America, Africa and the West Indies. In 1763, England won the Seven Years War (known in America as the French and Indian War) and gained all of Canada. England was successful primarily because she had a strong navy and a strong prime minister, Lord Chatham. Lord Chatham did many things for England, but he would not kow-tow to King George III. The King intensely disliked his Prime Minister and even called him "the blackest heart."

Englishmen had been settling in America since early in the 1600's. Although three-fifths of the American colonists were English when the Revolution began, there were also Scots, Irish, Dutch, French Huguenots, Germans, Swedes and Swiss living there too. Each of these groups brought new customs and ideas to America, and because the government in England had paid little attention to the colonies, they developed their own life and laws. But, when England went to war with other countries, her colonies loyally fought her enemies in America.

When the Seven Years War ended, England got enormous new territories and an equally enormous debt. The King, and many of his subjects, felt that Americans should both help pay the debt and contribute to their own defense particularly along the Indian frontiers. So, the King decided to levy new taxes on the colonists.

Though the colonies recognized the King's authority in some things, they did not recognize his right to make them pay taxes they had not voted for. Lord Chatham, a warm friend of the colonies, put it this way, "No subject of England shall be taxed but by his own consent."

And the colonists echoed this when they cried, "No taxation without representation."

Because the British treasury was low, King George's government paid little attention to the complaints of the colonists. They imposed more and more taxes—taxes on sugar, silk, calico and wine. They even passed a Stamp Act. This meant that no document could be legal until a stamp purchased from the government had been placed upon it. As the taxes grew in number, the colonists became angrier and angrier. They rioted. They attacked the homes of British officials in America. Finally they refused to purchase from England any of the taxed articles.

When the British merchants began to lose more money in lost trade than the government made in taxes, they criticized the taxes too. Gradually many were removed.

In 1773 Parliament declared a new tax—a tax on tea. The colonists protested. They said no tea was to land in their ports,

Colonial cartoon

5

and if it were landed it would be put in warehouses and not sold. In Boston alone the authorities refused to take any notice of the colonists' protests.

That is why Boston men dressed up as Indians, masked themselves with black soot and dumped the tea into Boston Harbor—£18,000 sterling worth of tea!

The British Government was now very angry. One Member of Parliament said the people of Boston "ought to be knocked about their ears and destroyed."

As punishment, Parliament passed the Coercive Acts. (Colonists called them the Intolerable Acts.) The government of Massachusetts lost many of its liberties. The capital was moved from Boston to Salem. Town meetings were restricted. Boston Harbor was closed to all shipping, even ferryboats.

A military governor, General Thomas Gage, was sent from England. He was ordered not to restore any of Boston's freedoms until the £18,000 sterling (about $90,000) worth of tea was paid for.

Many people in England were shocked by this harshness, especially members of the Whig party such as the former Prime Minister, Lord Chatham, Charles James Fox and Edmund Burke, the Irish-born orator. Burke, in particular, was the colonists' champion. He warned that the Coercive Acts were causing "a fierce spirit of liberty" to grow in America. He urged again and again that the stern laws be repealed and the colonists conciliated.

Boston had sympathizers in many other American colonies. When the Boston Port Bill (closing Boston Harbor) came into effect in June 1774 they sent food and supplies to the Bostonians. Virginia sent Indian corn; Maryland, pork, rye and bread; New Hampshire, cows and money.

People on both sides of the Atlantic were amazed. Until now the colonies had rarely agreed on anything and were jealous and distrustful of one another. King George and his ministers had never dreamed that the other twelve colonies would rally behind Massachusetts against the Crown.

One reason for this widespread support was the growth of Committees of Correspondence. A Massachusetts Rebel, Sam Adams, had founded them in 1772. Sam Adams was the perfect agitator, a man who loved the democracy of the New England town meeting. He worked ceaselessly for restoration to the colonies of "the true old English liberty which gives relish to every other enjoyment." He set up an effective system of letter-writers and post-riders. Whenever the British did anything that annoyed the local Rebels, the Committees wrote long letters about it and sent them racing to the other cities, and correspondents in all the colonies. This constant exchange

Lord Chatham

of news did much to keep the revolutionary spirit alive and organize opposition to the new laws. It was their substitute for telegraph and radio!

Also, in every colony, revolutionary parliaments called Provincial Congresses were set up. The colony of Virginia, second only to Massachusetts in revolutionary zeal, urged large annual meetings of delegates from all of the Congresses.

So, in September 1774, the delegates to the First Continental Congress met. They met in the largest city in America, and the second largest in the British Empire, Philadelphia, in Pennsylvania colony.

Every colony was represented at the First Continental Congress except Georgia. Virginia sent a stately army officer and landowner, George Washington. From Pennsylvania came an old astute diplomat and inventor, Benjamin Franklin. Sam Adams and his cousin John, the lawyer, represented Massachusetts.

Edmund Burke

The Provincial Congresses also reorganized the militia, or local bands of volunteer soldiers in each colony. They got rid of any officer who did not agree with them politically. They started companies of young, very active soldiers called Minute Men. (Named so because they could spring to arms in a minute.)

The Provincial Congresses also ordered that ammunition and supplies be collected and stored in places of safety. Massachusetts' largest depot was in Concord, a town about eighteen miles from Boston. There the New England Rebels hid axes, medicine, gunpowder, candles, wine and raisins, all important to eighteenth-century warfare.

The **TIMES** are **Dreadful, Dismal Doleful Dolorous,** and **DOLLAR-LESS.**

From the Pennsylvania Journal, *1765*

Boston's Battlefields

*W*hen General Thomas Gage, the new military governor, arrived in Boston on May 13, 1774, he hoped he was coming as a peacemaker. He had lived for eighteen years in the colonies. He had an American wife, and was a Whig who had long disapproved of the King's policies toward his American subjects.

General Gage, however, did not understand one important result of the French and Indian War. Since the French were no longer in Canada to threaten them, the Massachusetts men were beginning to feel that they no longer needed England for protection. This made them all the more ready to oppose restrictions.

Before he left England, Gage had told the government that he was sure 1,500 soldiers were all he would need to restore order. After one summer of trying to rule the resentful Bostonians, he sent back a different message. If the government thought they should send 10,000 men, they had better send 20,000! If they had planned on giving him one million pounds, make it two!

But he got little support from the King and his advisers. They disagreed completely among themselves. The King was for severity. Lord North, his Prime Minister, wanted to make peace.

So Gage kept on grimly in Boston, trying to maintain order. He could not do much but his spies told him about the ammunition and other supplies growing daily in Concord. They, at least, could be destroyed. Under cover of night, on April 18, 1775, he sent six British companies out from Boston toward Concord.

But the Rebels had spies too. One of the most active was a gifted silversmith named Paul Revere. He was also one of the post-riders who carried letters for the Committees of Correspondence.

When the Rebel leaders heard that Gage's troops were on the move, they suspected that Concord was in danger. They were also worried lest the British capture, in nearby Lexington, two leading Boston revolutionaries, old Sam Adams, an

the rich young John Hancock. They asked Paul Revere and *Boston in peacetime*
a friend of his, William Dawes, to spread a warning through-
out the countryside.

Both men carried the message, but because Henry Wads-
worth Longfellow, a New England poet, wrote a long poem
in 1863 about Paul Revere, Revere is far more famous than
Dawes.

Revere was rowed across the Charles River. He borrowed
a horse and then by moonlight set out at a gallop on the
road toward Lexington. Dodging British patrols, he reached
Lexington, alarming "almost every house" on the way. Adams
and Hancock were warned of their danger. Then Dawes,
Revere and a Dr. Prescott, who was out late courting his girl,
started for Concord with the news "The redcoats are coming!"

Revere was captured by a patrol. While he was being taken
back to Boston, he escaped, lost his horse, and made his way
to safety on foot.

As a post-rider for Committees of Correspondence, Revere
was to carry many important messages all through the Revolution, but none was more important or famous than the one
he carried from Boston to Lexington that night. He may have
lost the horse, but the Minute Men were warned. Early the
next morning, six companies of redcoats marched on to

9

Lexington Green, where a band of armed and determined farmers met them.

"Disperse, ye rebels," the British commanding officer, Major John Pitcairn, ordered. A gun went off. No one knows for sure to this day who fired the first shot of the American Revolution, an English soldier or an American farmer. Both sides had been strictly ordered not to shoot.

Eight of the American militia died in the gunfire that followed, and ten were wounded. The rest scattered. The British companies marched on to Concord. They destroyed whatever supplies had not already been hidden by Americans.

Then the weary march back to Boston began. From behind every rock, tree and wall, American farmers shot at the British soldiers. By the time the troops reached the city, 273 men out of a redcoat force of 1,800 had fallen.

For several years the Rebel agitators had been organizing the Sons of Liberty in most of the towns and cities. They were groups of men and boys who used any new British tax law or regulation as an excuse to riot and attack the homes of British officials and those who sided with the government.

When the Massachusetts Committee of Correspondence sent word of the doings at Lexington and Concord through the colonies, blaming the British for firing first, whether they did or not, the Sons of Liberty ran rampant. They stormed the houses of people on the British side, tarring and feathering the owners. They threatened the British governors who fled from them to British warships. Volunteer soldiers from all over New England hurried toward the Rebel camp out-

*Concord and Lexington
April 18–19, 1775*

side Boston. Soon the city was under a siege nine miles long.

Early in May the New Englanders struck in another direction. Near the Canadian border, at Ticonderoga, between Lake George and Lake Champlain, there was a tumbledown fort.

A band of outlaws under a giant leader, Ethan Allen (they called themselves the Green Mountain Boys from their home in the Green Mountains of New Hampshire) set out to capture Fort Ticonderoga. On the way Allen was joined by a fiery, energetic Connecticut apothecary (druggist), turned army captain, Benedict Arnold.

Allen's Green Mountain Boys captured the forty-five redcoats in Ticonderoga "in the name of the Great Jehovah and the Continental Congress," surprising them while they slept.

With Ticonderoga the Americans had gained an important strategic point on the road to Canada. Better still, they captured sorely needed cannon. These were the guns that the following December Washington was to send north for —guns that in March 1776 forced the British to give up Boston.

Late in May General Gage's long-awaited reinforcements reached Boston—6,600 men under three British generals: Sir William Howe, Sir Henry Clinton and John Burgoyne.

Howe and Clinton knew the colonies well. Howe had fought in the French and Indian War. He was also a Whig who had been re-elected to Parliament in 1774, on the promise that he would refuse any command against the American

The Battle of Lexington engraving by Amos Doolittle

11

colonists. But when orders came to go to Boston to oppose the Rebels he obeyed, like a good soldier.

Sir Henry Clinton had grown up in New York City where his father had been governor for ten years. Burgoyne was a good soldier but also a great dandy. His troops called him Gentleman Johnny.

All three generals arrived in Boston eager to end the siege. Their plan was to fortify some of the heights surrounding the city. However, General Artemas Ward, elderly commander of the New England troops, got wind of the plan and moved first.

Two small hills rose on the Charleston peninsula near Boston, General Ward ordered that the taller one, Bunker Hill, should be fortified. But it was on the smaller, Breed's Hill, that Colonel William Prescott's men built their small fort. They had gone out after dark and worked all through the night to build it.

Next morning Boston was dumbfounded. The evening before, Breed's Hill had been empty. Now it had earthworks alive with digging soldiers.

There is a story that General Gage sent for one of his Loyalist councilors, Abijah Willard. He pointed to the hill. "Do you know that tall man on the parapet?" he asked.

Willard peered through the general's spy glass. "It is Colonel William Prescott, my brother-in-law."

"Will he fight?"

"I cannot answer for his men, but he will fight you to the gates of Hell."

"The fort must be captured!" General Gage said firmly.

Engagement at North Bridge in Concord, Doolittle engraving

Ships of war in Boston harbor

Prescott had chosen a place that could have been cut off easily, if British troops had landed behind it.

But the professional soldiers in Gage's council simply couldn't believe that raw, untrained farmers would stand up to a head-on attack from British regulars.

So in the mid-afternoon of June 17, led by General Howe himself, the British regiments, sweating under heavy packs, toiled in slow march up the hill directly facing the fort.

An order had been given the Rebels: "Don't fire until you see the whites of their eyes." So they waited.

When the British were only fifty yards away the Rebels fired. Twice the redcoat lines broke and were driven back, leaving piles of wounded and dead. When they returned the third time, the Americans had no more gunpowder. "Their fire went out like an old candle." The British took the fort with a bayonet charge, the retreating Americans wielding their musket butts like clubs.

Howe had succeeded in capturing Breed's Hill but at the cost of 1,000 killed or wounded. The Americans lost only 400—and one alone was from Boston.

Back in England there was horror at the size of the British losses. Sir William Eden told the Prime Minister, "Eight more such victories and we shall have no one left to report them."

The Battle of Bunker Hill (the name it was given although

13

it was fought over Breed's Hill) showed that untrained militia could stand up to trained soldiers. General Howe always remembered Bunker Hill's slaughter with such bitterness that although he personally was a very brave man and a fine strategist, he never again would attack an American fortified position. Though he won many battles he never followed them up, but delayed until his enemy could slip away. No one knows why—natural laziness or Whig sympathies? But possibly it was because Howe behaved like this that Britain lost her American colonies.

After Bunker Hill, Gage made no more attempts against the besieging New Englanders. This may be because of the great casualties he had suffered. He might well have succeeded if he had tried. The New England Army was disorganized, undisciplined, low in ammunition—and dwindling from desertions.

On June 14, the Second Continental Congress, then sitting in Philadelphia, took a momentous step. It adopted the New England Army outside of Boston. The next day it named a commander for the army. He was George Washington, a Virginia gentleman, veteran of the French and Indian War and a delegate to the Continental Congress. He was on horseback, on his way to Massachusetts to take over his new post, when he got the news of the Battle of Bunker Hill.

The main reason Congress chose Washington was a political one—he came from Virginia. Congress, however, could not have selected a better general. It did not seem so at first, for Washington made some almost fatal mistakes—but he learned from those mistakes.

As the Revolution dragged on year after year, Washington held together a hungry, ragged army, controlled jealous generals, coped with a stingy Congress. Most important— when he realized that he could never beat the British forces in America without the help of sea power, he refused to risk his small army in unnecessary battles until the French navy was on hand to help him. Unlike the generals opposing him, Washington saw just what he had to do to win the Revolution. When after six years of setbacks his chance for a decisive victory came, he seized it.

George Washington

14

Britain loses Boston but keeps Canada

*W*hen George Washington took over the forces surrounding Boston, he was disgusted by what he found. There was filth, disorder, little discipline, little ammunition and few supplies. He wrote his cousin, Lund, "They are an exceedingly dirty and nasty people," and set out sternly, with pillory and lash, to make soldiers of them.

Washington was convinced of the justice of the American position. He wrote to a friend, who was fearful at the way things were going, "I think the Parliament of Great Britain hath no more right to put their hands into my pocket, without my consent, than I have to put my hands into yours for money."

At the same time, he was one of the many Americans who blamed the Parliament and not the King for the troubles of the colonies. He was so sure at that time that the King would soon listen to his American subjects' complaints, that he wrote his wife, Martha, "I shall return safe to you in the fall."

But summer wore on into autumn, and autumn into winter. Sir William Howe inside Boston did nothing to break the siege, but neither did the Ministers in England seem ready to try to settle the dispute. In December, with most of his army threatening to go home when their enlistments ran out on the thirty-first, Washington thought of the great cannon that had been captured at Ticonderoga.

He promoted a fat young bookseller from Boston, Henry Knox, to Chief of Engineers, and sent him off to Ticonderoga to get the fifty guns. It was a tremendous job. The cannon had to be floated down Lake George and carried on sledges nearly 300 miles through the snowy New England mountains. It was almost February before the cannon reached Washington's headquarters. And when they came lumbering into camp there was not enough gunpowder for a full-scale bombardment of Boston!

Washington decided to act as General Artemas Ward had done before him. Under cover of night, on March 4, he sent out 3,000 men to build a fort on Dorchester Heights, south of the city. Again Bostonians awoke to find a fortification where there had been an empty hill the evening before. Only this time the great guns of Ticonderoga were aimed at the city's heart. (Several are still there!)

General Howe, who had replaced Gage, mustered his troops for an attack by sea on Dorchester Heights. Luckily for the Americans a hurricane came up. The attack had to be put off for several days. The Americans used the delay to build another fort even closer to Boston, on Nook's Hill.

Was it the memory of the slaughter of Bunker Hill that made Howe afraid to attack? He decided not to go for the American position on Dorchester Heights, but to pull out from Boston entirely and make Nova Scotia, in Canada, his next base.

But this meant more than just transporting troops. Hundreds of Americans loyal to the Crown had been flocking into Boston for safety ever since Concord and Lexington. Howe could not leave them behind for Rebel vengeance.

They were packed into the British ships in the harbor, bound as they said "For Hell, Hull, or Halifax." They were the first thousand of 100,000 Americans who went into exile rather than live outside the British Empire. They called themselves Loyalists. The Rebels called them Tories and traitors, often stole their goods, looted and confiscated the homes they left behind.

It was on St. Patrick's Day, March 17, 1776, that the British finally left Boston. They were unhindered by the Rebels. Howe warned Washington that he would set Boston afire if anyone tried to stop him from leaving with his army.

When the Americans pushed warily up to the deserted British lines, they found them quite empty, except for an occasional scarecrow draped in scarlet. About the neck of one hung a sign saying "Welcome, Brother Jonathan."

The next morning Washington rode into Boston. The siege was over! The city was in Rebel hands. But when and where would the British strike again?

While Washington was riding into a peaceful Boston, there was gunfire 600 miles to the north. In the summer of 1775, Congress had decided on a campaign against Canada. It had two good reasons. First, as long as Canada was in British hands New England and New York were in constant danger of invasion from the north. Second, the Americans had the true zeal of converts. In the enthusiasm of their rebellion they believed that the Canadians, too, must be ready to revolt against the Ministers of the King who, they believed, were taking their rights away.

Montgomery's Route to Quebec

16

An attack against Montreal was planned first. Sir Guy Carleton, commander of all British troops in Canada, had only 800 soldiers in the garrison in Montreal. The expedition was led by the energetic and experienced General Richard Montgomery. Ethan Allen, the New Hampshire man who had captured Fort Ticonderoga five months before, was sent ahead to persuade Canadians to enlist. Rashly he decided to attack Montreal on his own.

As his Green Mountain Boys advanced toward the city, Carleton's regulars sallied out. All but forty of the Americans turned and ran. Some fled a mile before they were captured. Allen was taken and sent in chains to England.

Allen's foolhardiness cost the Rebel cause much. Canadians who might have joined the Rebels, hesitated. The Loyalists remained convinced not only that it was right to remain loyal to Britain but that it was sensible. And the Indian tribes, who had not yet picked a side, chose the British as the winning one.

In spite of Allen's fiasco, Montgomery continued his march. On November 13, he took Montreal and its entire garrison. Only one soldier managed to escape; Sir Guy Carleton, the commanding officer, got away in a canoe.

Quebec was the next goal. There was to be a two-pronged approach. One, under Montgomery, would come from Ticonderoga. Benedict Arnold would lead a diversionary action. His troops were to travel up through Maine. With Arnold was another soldier, afterwards famous. He was a rifleman expert in Indian warfare, the huge Daniel Morgan.

Arnold's force of 1,100 started out through the cold wilderness. They forded swift rivers and carried their big flat boats and sixty-five tons of supplies around rapids. When it rained the men's clothes froze "a pane of glass thick." The boats stove in and leaked. The food rotted. In their starvation, Arnold's men devoured shoe leather, soap, candles, even their pet dogs. Arnold had miscalculated the distance greatly. By October 24, his army had traveled seven days longer than he had expected, and was not even halfway to Quebec!

Early in December Montgomery's men and Arnold's "famine-proof veterans," as they proudly called themselves, met outside Quebec's walls.

The two commanders faced a dilemma. They knew they had neither the time nor the strength to besiege Quebec. They must attack the city head on—though that would cost many lives. They also knew they must do it soon. On December 31, the New Englanders' enlistments would run out. Without the encouragement of a victory they would take their guns and start home.

Arnold's Route to Quebec

Quebec in 1777

Both Arnold and Montgomery agreed that if they must assault Quebec it would be safest to do it under cover of a snowstorm.

On the very last day of the year a "thick, small" snowstorm began. The Americans attacked. There was sharp street-fighting. Montgomery was killed and Arnold wounded. The invaders were driven back. Many escaped across the ice covering the Bay of St Charles, but about 400 were taken prisoner.

In spite of this defeat and his injuries, Arnold refused to give up. All winter he directed a siege of Quebec.

Smallpox broke out in his camp. Arnold was injured again by a fall from his horse. In May Sir Guy Carleton drove the Americans back across the St Lawrence. The Rebels, under a new commander, Major-General John Sullivan, withdrew to the head of Lake Champlain and the safety of Ticonderoga.

A Quebec Loyalist wrote, "Thus was the country freed from a swarm of misguided people, led by designing men, enemies of the liberties of the country, under the specious title of Assertors of American Rights."

The thirteen rebellious colonies had to accept the fact that Canada wanted to remain in the Empire, and that across her borders, at any time, the British could attack them.

18

Independence Declared

During the first year few, if any, Rebels fought for freedom from the Empire. In March 1775, Benjamin Franklin told Lord Chatham that he had never heard any American, drunk or sober, hint that he wanted a permanent separation from England.

Even the battles of Concord and Lexington did not mean an open break. While Congress was creating an army and launching an invasion into Canada, it still hoped for reconciliation. As John Adams put it: "Hold the sword in one hand and the olive branch in the other."

This was the mood in which the Second Continental Congress in the Summer of 1775 sent "The Olive Branch Petition" to King George.

Signed by forty-six delegates it was addressed to their "Most Gracious Sovereign." It said that the colonists earnestly wanted their "former harmony" and a "permanent reconciliation." In the meantime it asked that the killing of "Your Majesty's subjects" stop and the laws that distressed them be repealed.

King George refused to accept or read the petition. In August he proclaimed the Rebels "wicked and desperate persons" and urged their countrymen to inform on their "treasons and traitorous conspiracies." In December he followed up this Proclamation with the Prohibitory Acts. They stated that the colonies were no longer under British protection, all American ports would be blockaded and all American ships would be seized on the high seas.

The moderates in Congress were bitterly disappointed by the King's actions. As a Virginia delegate, Thomas Jefferson, wrote, "It is an immense misfortune to the whole empire to have a king of such a disposition at such a time." But the more fiery Rebels claimed that the King had now forced independence on them!

The colonies on the whole were now ready for the second document that would change the course of their history—a forty-seven-page pamphlet called *Common Sense*.

Common Sense was a highly emotional attack on the

British Government, the King and the idea of royalty itself. Written by Tom Paine, a political pamphleteer, ex-corset-maker and tax collector, its fiery message and rolling prose captured the colonial minds. It appeared in January 1776, and soon over 100,000 copies were circulating.

First, Tom Paine attacked the whole idea of having a king and then he went on to describe his ideal state (very unlike the one the United States has developed into) and ended with a dramatic last page. On a blank white sheet, in bold black letters appeared only seven words, "THE FREE AND INDEPENDENT STATES OF AMERICA." Cobblers, colonels, men, women, anyone who could read, read it. And as Washington said it worked a "powerful change in the minds of many men."

It pleaded with the American colonies to separate from the British Empire. Tom Paine wrote, "Everything that is right or reasonable pleads for separation. The blood of the slain, the weeping voice of Nature cries 'Tis time to part'." And a North Carolina newspaper reported that *Common Sense* "made independents of the majority of the country."

Six months later the rest of the country were made "independents" by the Second Continental Congress. The document that announced it was the Declaration of Independence.

It was drafted by Thomas Jefferson, the brilliant, quiet, red-haired young Virginian with "a happy talent for composition."

When his fellow delegates asked him to write it, he was unwilling. But New Englander Adams felt that a Virginian should write the Declaration as he had felt a Virginian should head the army—and thus insure Virginia's support for the New England-begun Revolution.

Thomas Jefferson worked away in a second-story parlor of the home of a German bricklayer in Philadelphia. He didn't want to work up people's feelings, as Tom Paine had done, but to place "the common sense of the subject in terms so plain and firm as to command assent," and to justify "the independent stand we are compelled to take."

His fellow Congressmen made plenty of criticisms, suggestions and revisions, but the document was approved unanimously, and was signed by John Hancock on July 4—by the other delegates in August and afterwards.

The Declaration is a successful attempt to justify the American Revolution. It uses ideas about laws and government that go far back into Greek, Roman and medieval times. It owes a great deal to the seventeenth-century English philosopher John Locke. It also succeeds in being what Jefferson said he wanted it to be, "an expression of the American mind."

Title page of Common Sense

Independence Hall where Declaration of Independence was signed

Here is the famous preamble:

When in the course of human events, it becomes necessary for one people to dissolve the political bands which have connected them with another and to assume among the powers of the earth the separate and equal station to which the laws of Nature and of Nature's God entitle them, a decent respect to the opinion of mankind requires that they should declare the causes which impel them to this separation.

We hold these truths to be self-evident, that all men are created equal, that they are endowed by their Creator with certain inalienable Rights, that among these are Life, Liberty and the pursuit of Happiness. That to secure these rights Governments are instituted among men deriving their just powers from the consent of the Governed.

The Declaration continues by stating that whenever a government becomes "destructive of these ends" the people have a right to alter or abolish it and to institute a new government.

Franklin's cartoon urging colonies to join together

Thomas Jefferson

It then lists twenty-seven abuses with which it accuses, not Parliament, not the royal Ministers, but King George III himself. It says that he refused assent to good laws, dissolved parliaments, obstructed justice, cut off their trade, took away their charters, burned their towns, deprived many of trial by jury. It goes through the list grimly and bitterly. Most of its charges were fair; some were not. The most important was "imposing Taxes on us without our Consent."

It was such a tax that caused the Boston Tea Party, the Intolerable Acts, Lexington and Concord, Bunker Hill. Because, as Lord Chatham had said almost two years before Independence was declared, "No subject of England shall be taxed but by his own consent."

This Declaration of Independence finally split the colonists clearly into two opposing parties, and each side had a name for itself and one for its enemies. Those who agreed with the Declaration called themselves Patriots, but to the opposite party they were Rebels. Those who remained loyal to the King and the British Government called themselves Loyalists, but to the other side they were Tories.

The Fight for New York City

*W*hile bells rang and bonfires blazed through the thirteen
colonies to celebrate the adoption of the Declaration
of Independence, in New York City, Washington was pre-
paring for a British attack.

Washington had been in New York since April 13, 1776.
Now in July, General Sir William Howe was sailing down
from Halifax in Canada with an army of well-trained troops,
while his brother, Admiral Lord Howe, was approaching
with a large fleet. Both English and American commanders
understood the strategic importance of New York. It lay between New England and the southern colonies: if one British
army could drive up the Hudson River from New York City
and join with another British army from Canada, between
them they could cut New England off from the rest of the
rebelling colonies. New York City could also be a base for
an attack on Philadelphia, the home of the American Congress.

Because he had no experience as a general, Washington
did not understand that in spite of the forts, cannons and
barricades bristling through all the city, nothing could stop
the British from taking it. New York City is on an island. It
lies on a great harbor. Deep wide rivers rim two of its sides.
A British fleet could capture it easily.

The British leaders had found it so hard to recruit Englishmen to fight against the Americans that King George had
hired German soldiers. People in both England and America
were very angry about this. The Rebels called all these soldiers "Hessians."

Washington should have moved his army out of New York
to the highlands of the Hudson River. From there he could
have blocked Howe from marching north or from striking
at Philadelphia. He made a big mistake. He tried to defend
Brooklyn Heights, across New York Harbor on Long Island.

On August 22, the Howe brothers landed a force on Long
Island. General Howe did not attempt a head-on assault on
Brooklyn Heights. He out-maneuvered Washington bril-

liantly, attacking the American flank after having found a way around by an unguarded road. The Americans were lured into the open and crushed. It was a very savage battle. The Hessians had been told that the Americans would kill all their prisoners, so they killed all the Americans they captured.

After his victory on Long Island, Sir William Howe did what he was going to do again and again during the Revolution. Nothing! Instead of following up his success he waited. He wasted several days.

While Howe waited, on the night of August 29th, Washington brought his army of 9,500 men safely across the East River from Brooklyn to New York. The army was rowed by a regiment of fishermen from Marblehead in Massachusetts. In heavy rain and thick fog, stealthily, the whole beaten army escaped out of Howe's trap.

Some historians believe that if the Declaration of Independence had not been adopted before the American defeat on Long Island, it might never have been adopted at all.

Both the Howes thought that the defeated Rebels must surely now sue for peace. (The Howes' chief wish was to make peace not war, anyway!) They wasted more time waiting to hear from Washington. Washington made no peace move.

He had decided at last that he must leave New York City. He was in the midst of moving his troops out when, on September 15, Howe struck again. This time the British at-

Washington's New York headquarters

tacked the middle of Manhattan Island at a place called Kip's Bay. (It is now about 34th Street and the East River.)

First there was cannonading. Then boatloads of redcoats landed. (A Rebel private said they looked like a "clover field in full bloom.") As the British invaded the island, halting part-way across it, the Americans fled. Washington became so angry at his troops' cowardice, he lost all self-control. Cursing, he hit about him with his riding-crop. In the daze that followed this outburst of temper he was almost captured.

It seemed as though the several thousand American soldiers caught in New York City south of Kip's Bay must be captured. But a Mrs. Robert Murray (a middle-aged mother of twelve, not the young beauty of American legend) invited Sir William into her house for wine and cake. While British soldiers waited outside in the broiling sun, the officers rested in Mrs. Murray's shady parlor. They rested just ten minutes too long to prevent the last Americans under General Israel Putnam from escaping!

Washington had brought his whole army safely out of Manhattan. Two days later a great fire broke out in the city he had given up so unwillingly. A quarter of the city was burned. The morning after the fire there was a sudden hanging. A Rebel captain, a schoolmaster from New Haven, Connecticut, named Nathan Hale, had volunteered to slip into the city for information. As he was leaving with his information, he was identified and captured. A contemporary newspaper reported that Hale, on suspicion of being a spy (and

American boats at anchor in the Narrows between Long Island and Staten Island, New York, Lord Howe approaching, 1776

New York harbor in 1757

of starting the fire), was "taken up and dragged without ceremony to the execution post and hung up." His words, "I only regret I have but one life to lose for my country," are among the most stirring in American history.

For almost a month, Howe left Washington alone on rocky Harlem Heights. The American army seemed about to collapse. There were hundreds of desertions. Washington lacked competent officers. He said his surgeons, for instance, "were very great rascals." General Henry Knox, who had brought the cannon from Ticonderoga to Boston, described the army outside of New York as a "receptacle for ragamuffins."

While Washington worked, watched and worried, Howe lagged. Finally, on October 28, 1776, he met and beat Washington once more, yet again he failed to follow up his victory.

Howe moved next against the two Hudson River strongholds north of New York, Fort Washington and Fort Lee. On the night of November 16, at Fort Washington, the Americans lost 2,800 men, 146 cannon and masses of ammunition. Three days later, in a dawn attack, Fort Lee, on the opposite side of the Hudson, was seized by Howe. As one British officer wrote: "The rebels fled like scared rabbits . . . they left some poor pork, a few greasy proclamations, and some of that scoundrel COMMON SENSE man's letters which we can read at our leisure now that we have got one of the

impregnable redoubts of Mr Washington to quarter in."
(New York City was to be held by the British until 1783!)

Washington and his army—now down to 3,000—were on
the run. Dodging through New Jersey, keeping one day's
march away from the British, the Rebels seemed, as one
redcoat put it, to be playing Bo Peep. Washington knew how
desperate his plight was. But he told one of his aides, "My
neck does not feel as if it were made for a halter."

By now many of Washington's critics and even his friends
began to doubt that he could win the war. He himself, when
he had accepted his generalship had said, "I do not think
myself equal to the command." Since he had arrived in
New York from Boston in April, Washington had lost skirmishes and battles, forts and cities. Five thousand of his men
were prisoners. His army had shrunk from 20,000 to 3,000.

One of his generals, Charles Lee, complained about Washington's failures. He was just finishing a letter in which he
said, "A certain great man is damnably deficient" when he
was captured—in dressing-gown and slippers—by a detachment of British dragoons! One of Lee's staff who had listened
to his complaining thought it was a trick to get over to the
British. "What a damn sneaking way of being kidnapped!"
he cried. But Washington, who depended heavily on General
Lee, wrote to Congress, "Our cause has received a severe
blow."

December 1776 was half over. Washington knew that unless he heartened his soldiers with a victory most of them would go home when their enlistments ran out on the thirty-first. He determined to try for such a victory.

Washington's plan included a Christmas night crossing of the ice-choked Delaware River, and an attack on the town of Trenton, New Jersey, which was held by the Hessian troops.

The regiment of blue-jacketed fishermen from Marblehead who had rowed the American Army to safety after the defeat on Long Island was again at the oars. Once across the Delaware River, despite raw cold and wild snow-storms, the troops, as General Knox wrote his wife, "marched with the most profound silence and good order."

The Hessian Colonel, Johannes Rall, and his men had been overcelebrating Christmas with rum and wine. The American attack roused their sentries from drunken sleep. Rall was slain. In forty-five minutes almost 1,000 prisoners were taken. There were only five American casualties.

After the battle, the Rebels marched back nine freezing miles in the storm and recrossed the Delaware. When their boat bottoms became caked with ice, both captors and prisoners jumped up and down, their pigtails flapping, until the ice fell off.

On the last day of the year, Washington urged his soldiers to re-enlist and the drum beat for volunteers. Not a man stepped forward. Washington said, "If you will consent to stay only one month longer, you will render that service to

Landing at Kip's Bay

the cause of liberty and your country which probably you never can do under any other circumstances." When the drums beat again, his whole gaunt, tattered army answered his appeal.

The victory at Trenton made the British call in another general. Lord Cornwallis arrived at Trenton on the night of January 2 and was advised to attack the Americans immediately. He said he could "just as well bag the fox next morning." His quartermaster said: "My Lord, if you trust these people tonight, you will see nothing of them in the morning." The quartermaster was right. Knowing the British outnumbered him, Washington muffled his cannon wheels, left his campfires burning, and led his army to Princeton.

In a short, fierce battle with some British troops at Princeton, the redcoats began to run. Washington spurred after them shouting: "It's a fine fox chase, my boys!" But he could not hold the town, for his men were weary and Cornwallis was near. Finally he withdrew his army to a mountain plateau in New Jersey where he could watch British movements in New York and guard the road between New England and Philadelphia.

His army, half-naked, worn out and stricken with smallpox, waited there for spring. Howe, in the comfort of New York, let them alone.

British forces under Cornwallis land at the New Jersey Palisades, drawing by Lord Rawdon

29

The Road to Saratoga

"John Burgoyne wagers Charles Fox one pony [about $250] that he will be home victorious from America by Christmas Day, 1777." So runs the first wager in an eighteenth-century betting-book in Brooks's Club in London.

Dashing General John Burgoyne had a plan to win the war against the Rebels. He described it in a paper he presented to King George III. The paper was called *Thoughts for Conducting the War from the Side of Canada*. The King and his ministers approved, so on May 6, 1777, Burgoyne arrived in Quebec, Canada, ready to put his plan into action.

It consisted of a three-pronged attack. One army (under Burgoyne) was to come down the Hudson River from Canada to Albany, a town at the center of the state, now the capital of the State of New York. The second army, under Barry St Leger, was to cross the Mohawk Valley from Oswego and meet Burgoyne at Albany. The third army (under General Howe) was to come up the Hudson River from New York City to Albany. When the three armies met, New England would be cut off from the remaining colonies.

On paper the plan seemed good. Its success, however, depended on two essentials. Clear commands must come from London coordinating Howe's and Burgoyne's moves. Howe and Burgoyne must work together and keep in touch with each other. But neither of these things happened. King George was badly served by his ministers, especially by Lord George Germain, Head of the Colonial Office, and in charge of the general plan of the war. It was partly his fault that the Burgoyne plan failed. Some historians say that he did not send the proper orders to America because he was in a hurry to start his holiday. Others say he sent contradictory orders to Burgoyne and Howe.

First, Germain approved Burgoyne's plan but shortly afterwards he approved a different plan of General Howe's. Howe wanted to move against Philadelphia instead of marching north to Albany. Since Germain had no understanding of the difficulties of wilderness warfare in America, he may have thought Howe could first take Philadelphia and then

General John Burgoyne

30

go to Burgoyne's help in the north before the winter began.

Burgoyne was told nothing of Howe's new plan. When, in June 1777, he started down the Great Lakes toward Albany, he believed that Howe was on his way to meet him.

Ticonderoga was easily captured by Burgoyne—a great blow to the Rebels, who then retreated to Fort Edward with Burgoyne following close behind. In his efforts to catch up with the Rebels, Burgoyne made his first serious mistake. A Loyalist adviser, Philip Skene, persuaded him to take his army by land instead of water. (Skene had property in the area so he wanted the British to build a road there.)

Burgoyne plunged into the swampy, pathless forests. The route was made harder because Rebels felled giant pines to block the path, destroyed bridges and scattered boulders in his way. Soon Burgoyne's army was completely bogged down. With its forty-two pieces of heavy artillery it could advance only one mile a day. Supplies were running out, and mosquitoes and flies were a black plague.

The Rebel commander, General Philip Schuyler, had crippled Burgoyne's advance, but his forces were not strong. There were few local volunteers. Then a crime by two of Burgoyne's Red Indians turned the local farmers over to the Rebel side. The Indians killed and scalped a young girl engaged to a Tory officer. When one of them returned to the British camp with Jane McCrea's scalp in his belt, Burgoyne did not punish him. He feared the other Indians would resent it and desert if he did. This, of course, angered everyone. "Remember Jane McCrea" became a frontier war-cry. Farmers seized their muskets and set out to join Schuyler.

While Burgoyne's ponderous army was lumbering south to Albany, Colonel Barry St Leger was leading the second prong of the attack up the Mohawk Valley. When he reached a small log fort on the Mohawk River, Fort Stanwix (where the city of Rome, New York, is now) he demanded its surrender. But the valley men inside the fort ran up no white flag. Instead they raised a banner the British had never seen before. It had thirteen red and white stripes and a circle of thirteen white stars on a dark blue field. It was the new American flag. It had been designed by George Washington and a fashionable Philadelphia dressmaker, Betsy Ross.

The women inside Fort Stanwix had read a description of the newly-designed flag in a newspaper. They made this one from a red petticoat, a white shirt and an officer's blue coat. Over the little frontier fort of Fort Stanwix, the Star Spangled Banner was flown for the first time in battle. St Leger surrounded Fort Stanwix with his regulars and war-whooping Indians and laid siege to it. The fort refused to

General Sir William Howe

31

Frontier settlement in the Mohawk Valley

The first American flag

give in. A prosperous farmer, General Nicholas Herkimer, who lived in a big red house on the Mohawk River, set out with 800 volunteers to break the siege. He was ambushed near a ravine in Oriskany. His horse was shot from under him. His leg was shattered. Although mortally wounded, propped up against a tree trunk, he directed the battle. The Mohawk Valley militia formed a circle around him in the woods, and with knife and musket, pistol and tomahawk, drove the Indians off.

Two weeks later General Benedict Arnold (the Connecticut apothecary who had led the campaign into Canada) arrived to help Fort Stanwix. He had only 950 soldiers, none of them from the district around, so he decided to trick St Leger into thinking he was far stronger than he was. Arnold persuaded Hon Yost, a feeble-minded boy, to go into St Leger's camp with news that a great Rebel army was coming. (They shot bullet-holes in Hon Yost's jacket to support the tale.)

When Hon ran into St Leger's camp and the Indians asked how many Americans were coming, he babbled and pointed to the leaves on the trees. Three Indians, secretly friendly

32

to the Rebels, followed with even more frightening stories
of the vast army approaching.

An Indian chief approached St Leger. He said: "When
we marched down you told us there would be no fighting
for us Indians. We might go down and smoke our pipes, but
now a number of our warriors have been killed and you
mean to sacrifice us." Despite St Leger's protests, the chief
departed with 800 men. St Leger had to give up the siege.

In the meantime, Burgoyne was getting desperately short
of food. The Americans had destroyed everything that could
feed his army. All corn had been laid waste, all cattle driven
off. On August 20 Burgoyne wrote a bitter letter to Lord
George Germain. He complained that the Loyalists did not
help him enough. He grumbled because he could not get in
touch with Howe. His messengers, he wrote, had been caught
by the Rebels and hanged. He ended gloomily: "I little
foresaw I was to be left to pursue my way through such a
tract of country without any co-operation from New York."

By September, Burgoyne knew that Howe was definitely
on his way to Philadelphia instead of coming to meet him.

A British camp

*British cartoon showing
General Howe doing
nothing*

He could expect no help. Burgoyne faced a cruel choice. Should he attack on his own and reach Albany before winter? Should he retreat to the safety of Ticonderoga? Burgoyne, always a gambler, decided to attack.

On September 13 and 14, he crossed to the west bank of the Hudson River and prepared to move against the Rebel posts. His spy system was poor. His Indians were deserting. There were 7,000 Americans commanded by Horatio Gates (who had replaced Schuyler) against Burgoyne's 6,000 soldiers. Militia had swarmed in from all over New England and New York. General Benedict Arnold was back. Washington had sent up Colonel Daniel Morgan and his sharpshooters. Every day the American army grew.

Under the guidance of the brilliant Polish engineer, Thaddeus Kosciusko, the Americans had built strong defenses. Burgoyne attacked head-on. Morgan's rifles repulsed him. Three weeks later there was another unsuccessful assault by Burgoyne. He had now lost 1,200 men. As he tried to retreat to Saratoga, he was followed by an army three times the size of his, for more militia kept joining the American side. Burgoyne's food was running out.

On October 7, 1777, the two armies met and Burgoyne was thrown back. Benedict Arnold, who had been confined to his tent after a dispute with General Gates, rushed out, leaped on a borrowed horse, and led the charge. Burgoyne's men were driven back, suffering losses five times the Americans'. Arnold was shot in the same leg that had been injured at Quebec.

Two days later Burgoyne retreated to Saratoga. Swarming like birds of prey, American militia pushed behind him, cutting off his escape. He despaired of help from Clinton. On October 17, Burgoyne surrendered. Clinton, coming to help him, heard the bad news and returned to New York.

But where was General Howe during the summer of 1777, when Burgoyne thought he was coming north to help him? He was planning a campaign to take Philadelphia, "the

Rebel capital." Washington tried to stop him but finally Howe tricked him into marching north—out of the way. At last the road to Philadelphia was clear of Americans! Unhindered, Howe marched into Philadelphia on September 26. But once there, he did very little else. He had captured the city but failed to destroy Washington's army. He had left Burgoyne alone to lose seven generals, 300 officers and over 5,000 men at Saratoga. Howe could win battles—he never lost one to Washington—but he never managed to get real results from his victories.

Saratoga is one of the decisive battles of history. After it, the British gave up hope of a successful invasion of the colonies from Canada. More important, France, who had been helping America secretly, now came openly to her aid.

On February 6, 1778, France recognized the new republic. She signed a treaty promising full military support to the United States. She declared war on England. Spain and Holland followed her example a year later.

When the King's ministers in London heard about Burgoyne's surrender, Lord North presented the Conciliatory Proposals to Parliament. Almost every American grievance was removed—even Parliament's claim to the right to tax the colonies. Lord North said that there was so much affection left in the colonies for England, "that barely to enter on the discussion was half the business."

It was not easy for Lord North to persuade Parliament to agree to the Conciliatory Proposals. Many members thought their corrupt and incompetent rulers, having lost them an army at Saratoga and dragged them into a World War, were panicking instead of facing up to danger.

Lord Chatham, America's great champion, though desperately ill, dragged himself to Parliament and gave a stirring speech. He first attacked the dismemberment "of this ancient and noble monarchy." He attacked the Tory government for using German mercenaries against American colonials. He said, "My lords, if I were an American, as I am an Englishman, while a foreign troop was landed in my country I never would lay down my arms—never, never, never." When he tried to speak again he collapsed and was carried out, to die a month later.

A few months earlier America might have accepted North's offer, but now she refused. The victory at Saratoga and the French treaty made the change. America now had a powerful ally and a European fleet to help her. England was suddenly caught in another World War in which her American colonial campaigns were only a small part. That was what gunfire at Lexington had brought England to—World War.

British cartoon: The horse America throwing her master

France Comes In

*F*rance's entry into the war in February 1778 was the result of much plotting by American diplomats whom Congress had sent to Paris. The aim of the Americans in Europe was to stir up European powers against England, and to get the help of a foreign navy.

Early in the war, Congress set up two committees for this purpose. The first, the Secret Committee, under a merchant, Robert Morris, organized the already widespread smuggling of European goods to America. The second, the Committee of Secret Correspondence, hired spies and tried to find foreign allies. This second Committee was headed by Benjamin Franklin, a plain, seventy-year-old scholar, writer and scientist. He was used to Europe; for eighteen years he had been a colonial agent in London.

After the defeat of Long Island and the retreat through New Jersey, the French began to doubt if America could win. Shrewd old Franklin argued with the Comte de Vergennes, France's foreign minister. He told Vergennes that when France helped America, she was just getting her revenge for the beating in the Seven Years War. He reminded Vergennes that if America lost the Revolution, the British Empire would be stronger than before. Vergennes saw Franklin's point.

Besides money and supplies, Europe sent experienced army officers who volunteered to fight for the Rebels. Some were self-seeking fortune-hunters; many did great deeds for America. The French Louis du Portail and Polish Thaddeus Kosciusko were clever engineers. Casimir Pulaski, another Pole, organized the first American cavalry regiment. Baron Wilhelm von Steuben reorganized and trained the whole army during the winter at Valley Forge. Most famous and loved of all was the young Frenchman, the Marquis de Lafayette. He became a major-general in the American army at twenty-one but never took a penny for his services.

When, on December 1, 1777, news of the victory of Saratoga finally reached Paris, the French cheered in their streets and squares "as if it had been a victory of their own troops over their own enemies." Vergennes now realized that Eng-

Benjamin Franklin

land would probably try to make peace with her colonies. She might even offer them independence. He wrote to the French ambassador in Madrid, "The power that first recognizes the independence of the Americans will be the one to gather all the fruits of the war." The next day the Crown Council of France agreed to the alliance and Vergennes told Franklin that France would enter the war openly.

Although the American–French treaty was signed in February 1778, it was May before the news could reach America. During the long cold months, Washington's army shivered and starved in their winter camp in Valley Forge. Many of the troops had no shoes, breeches, stockings or blankets. Since the camp had to be fortified before huts could be built, the men froze in tattered tents well into January. As Washington wrote to Congress, they "occupy a cold, bleak hill and sleep under frost and snow." Since soap and water were as scarce as food and clothes, their sores festered and bodies itched.

Much of this tragic suffering was unnecessary. Food shortages were due to mismanagement and inefficiency. There was grain in the Pennsylvania countryside, but no wagons to haul it into camp; there was meat, but no salt to keep it from rotting. Congress, driven out of Philadelphia by Howe, was torn with disagreements. But, while Congressmen bickered and blundered, the men at Valley Forge went barefoot in the snow and supped "as usual on a leg of nothing and no turnips." One of the reasons for this mismanagement was the weakness of the government. In November 1777, Congress had drawn up a plan for a confederation of the states called *The Articles of Confederation and Perpetual Union.* This confederation, hardly more than a "league of friendship," was fatally weak because it did not give Congress power to enforce laws over the thirteen states or to get things done. Worst of all, Congress could not levy taxes. It had no way of raising money to run the government well. So it could never feed, clothe or pay the men in the army properly. That is why there was so much grumbling, suffering and even mutiny in the army as the war went on.

But Washington's army survived the winter. Indeed, they marched out of Valley Forge far better soldiers than they had marched in. This was because a German volunteer, Wilhelm von Steuben, had been training them. He was a bald, big-nosed Prussian officer who had been fifteen years out of work when Benjamin Franklin met him in Paris and sent him to Washington. He set up drill teams, reorganized the army, wrote a handbook of arms. He spoke no English and when his soldiers could not understand his commands, he

Paper money issued by Congress, engraved by Paul Revere

begged his interpreters to "come and swear for me in English."

How well von Steuben understood American soldiers is shown in a letter to a friend in Europe: "In the first place the genius of this nation is not in the least to be compared with that of Prussians, Austrians and French. You say to your soldier 'Do this,' and he does it, but I am obliged to say 'This is the reason why you ought to do that' and then he does it."

Washington made a second important appointment in Valley Forge. In March 1778, Nathanael Greene became Quartermaster-General. Greene was a soldierly, industrious, intelligent, husky man, with a limp. His efficiency meant that starving soldiers now ate, and naked ones were clothed.

With May came the news of the French treaty. Washington said, "I believe no event was ever received with more heartfelt joy," and prepared for his summer campaign.

In March 1778, Howe, who had wintered comfortably in Philadelphia, heard that Sir Henry Clinton was replacing him as General. On his arrival in Philadelphia, Clinton got orders to abandon the city, since it could not be held against the expected French fleets. He planned to retreat to New York by land, fearing that if he went by sea the French might attack him. In June 1778, the long files of British soldiers started out from Philadelphia. Heavily laden, marching in the broiling sun, they were a tempting target.

General Lee (the officer who had been captured by the British in dressing-gown and slippers) was now back with Washington after a winter as a prisoner in New York. He had only lately been exchanged and did not realize what von Steuben's training had done for the army at Valley Forge. Washington sent Lee to attack the British near Monmouth. Lee did not attack as he had been ordered because he thought Clinton's troops were too strong. His men began to retreat, then to run. Washington sent a messenger to ask why. There is a story that when he returned, Washington galloped forward, angrily asking why Lee had not attacked. "Sir, these troops are not able to meet British Grenadiers!" "Sir," Washington thundered, "they are able and by God they will!" A Virginia general said later of Washington: "Sir, he swore on that day till the leaves shook on the trees. Sir, on that ever memorable day, he swore like an angel from heaven."

Washington stopped the retreat and rallied the men, and there was a sharp battle. That night Washington slept on the field. He planned to continue the battle next day. But while he slept, Clinton's army stole away to New York.

General Charles Lee

Sea Battles and
Indian Warfare

*Captain John
Paul Jones*

*F*rom the March day in 1776 when Washington watched
General Howe sail safely away from Boston, and then
again safely into New York Harbor in July 1776, he longed
for the help of a European navy. Now that France had come
into the war on the American side, and a French fleet was
on its way across the Atlantic, Washington had high hopes
of ending the war. He believed that if an American army
and a French fleet together launched an attack against the
British, victory could be had.

Great Britain now hoped to end the war too—by con-
ciliation. In June 1778, the Earl of Carlisle arrived in Philadelphia with peace offers from Parliament granting almost
everything the colonists had demanded at the start of the
war. There would be no standing army in the colonies. There
would be no changes in colonial charters unless America
wanted them. Either Americans could send representatives
to Parliament, or if preferred, Congress would be recognized
as an American Parliament. Most important, there would be
no taxation without representation.

The President of Congress, Henry Laurens, said: "If all
the fine things now offered had been offered some time ago"
there is no doubt they would have been accepted. But now,
"they seem to mistake our understanding as once they did
our resolution." Even Carlisle himself soon saw how useless
his efforts were. "The leaders on the enemy's side are too
powerful," he wrote his wife, "the common people hate us
in their hearts."

Less than a month after Congress rejected the Carlisle
offer, the French fleet arrived outside of New York Harbor.
Washington was overjoyed. The French had three times the
British firing power. They could sail into the Harbor and destroy the British fleet lying at anchor there. But the French
Admiral, Charles d'Estaing, was afraid that his big ships
would run aground on the sand bar that blocked the mouth
of the Harbor. He refused to try to cross it.

When, after ten days of discussion, Washington saw that

40

the French would not attack the British fleet at New York he persuaded d'Estaing to move against the second most important British-held seaport in America—Newport, in Rhode Island. D'Estaing began the siege, but gave it up after a hurricane, known as the "Great French Storm," damaged his ships. Angry at American criticism, he sailed away to the West Indies. During these two unsuccessful attempts at a joint American land and French sea action against the British, Washington had withdrawn to White Plains near New York. He was in the same position he had held in 1776 before his retreat across New Jersey. He was to spend the rest of the war in this district, refusing to risk his army and waiting for another chance for a decisive blow in cooperation with a French fleet.

The most effective sea weapons the Americans had against the British were privateers, or privately owned sea raiders. During the Revolution 2,000 American raiders destroyed $18,000,000 worth of British ships and cargoes. British merchants lost so much that many became eager for the war's end. The most famous American privateer was a Scottish-born sea captain, John Paul Jones. During the war he sailed up and down the English Channel attacking merchant ships and seaports and then returning to French or Dutch harbors for safety.

Jones's most famous victory took place in the North Sea.

His Majesty's ships under attack, engraving by Leon Elliott

41

He commanded the *Bonhomme Richard,* an ancient Indiaman supplied by the French. (Its name was a French translation of Poor Richard, Benjamin Franklin's pen name.)

The *Bonhomme Richard,* and three small ships with her, attacked a British convoy which was being escorted by two British men-o'-war, the *Serapis* and the *Countess of Scarborough.* The convoy escaped. Jones maneuvred his ship close to the *Serapis* and lashed the two ships together. All night they fought; at times both were in flames. When the *Bonhomme Richard* seemed to be sinking and the British captain summoned Jones to surrender, Jones answered: "I have not yet begun to fight!" At dawn the *Serapis'* powder magazine blew up. Her guns were wrecked and everyone behind the mainmast killed. Her captain surrendered and "the two captains now withdrew into the cabin and there drank a glass or two of wine together." Two days later, the war-torn *Bonhomme Richard* sank in the North Sea.

Just as American privateers harried British shipping all through the Revolution, so Indian braves harried the American frontier settlements. In those days the western frontier stretched in a long curve from Maine southward to Georgia. Over it the Indian menace hung "like a scythe of death."

The Indians bitterly resented how the Americans kept moving westward, clearing the ground, building cabins and destroying ancient Indian hunting grounds. So most Indians were allies of the British during the Revolution, attacking and destroying the lonely frontier homes and families of the Americans. People in both England and America condemned the use of Indians in the war. But, although the British used the Indians much more than the Americans did, they were not the first to do it. There were Indians among the Minute Men in the battle of Lexington. In 1775 Congress told its Indian Commissioners to try to keep the Indians neutral or else enlist them on the American side. But, because the British gave more in the way of gifts and promises and because at first it looked as if the British would win the war, the Indian chieftains sided with the British and their Tory allies.

Indians marched with Burgoyne to Saratoga. Indians were with St Leger during the siege of Fort Stanwix—and left him after Oriskany. The British Army never did—or perhaps never could—use Indians very sensibly. In the long run Indians probably did more harm than good to the British side. Their sneak raids, scalpings and burnings turned many frontiersmen against the British and Tories.

One of the most dramatic campaigns against the Indians was led by a tall, young, red-haired surveyor and experienced

Cherokee Indian warrior

fighter, George Rogers Clark, against the southern Indian tribes. The British supply base for these Indians was Fort Detroit, commanded by Colonel Henry Hamilton.

Lonely frontier log cabin

In June 1778, Clark organized a band of 170 Virginia frontiersmen. He floated them down the Ohio River and led them on a 120-mile march to French-held Kaskaskia, now in the State of Illinois. When the French settlers heard about the American–French treaty they agreed to help Clark. He captured several French towns, including Vincennes in present-day Indiana.

In December, in a swirling snowstorm, Hamilton re-took Vincennes. Clark said "an enemy could not suppose we should be so mad as to attempt to march eighty leagues through a drowned country in the depth of winter." They would be off their guard and "not think it worthwhile to keep out spies." So he marched his 170 men through flooded stretches of icy water, sometimes shoulder-deep. When he finally recaptured Vincennes, Clark cold-bloodedly executed some Indian captives while their tribesmen looked on—to convince the tribesmen that the British could not protect them. He then claimed territory more than half the size of all thirteen colonies, for Virginia.

Iroquois Indian country

Another much larger campaign was organized by Congress in 1779 against one of the most powerful Indian tribes—the Six Nations of the Iroquois. General John Sullivan led the campaign. Sullivan's expedition was in revenge for the Tory and Indian raids.

In July 1778, Tory Colonel John Butler, with 500 Senecas, had attacked Wyoming Valley in Pennsylvania, destroying a thousand homes. In September, Indians wiped out a Mohawk Valley village. Then in November Tories and Indians attacked Cherry Valley, a village about fifty miles west of Albany, New York.

Sullivan was sent to stop such raids. Washington ordered him: the country of the Six Nations must not be "merely overrun but destroyed." He led 5,000 men through 400 miles of wilderness, aiming to capture Fort Niagara—the main British supply base for the Iroquois.

On August 29, 1779, in Newtown, near Elmira, New York, Sullivan beat an army of Indians and Tories. He burned more than forty Indian towns; laid hundreds of acres of grain and orchards to waste. Hundreds of Iroquois died of disease and starvation the next winter. He could not, however, reach Fort Niagara, and so failed to cut off the Iroquois war-making power at its source. In 1780, the Iroquois survivors were back on the warpath. Blazing with revenge, they looted and killed more savagely than before.

The sprawling frontier still lived in terror of Indian raids.

44

The Sword in the South

*T*he treaty with France brought the French into open war against England in February 1778. A year later Spain and Holland also entered the war on the American side. With three European powers and America united against her, England began to show the stout heart that has carried her through world wars ever since. She started an attack in the southern states. She used her Loyalist volunteers more successfully.

In November 1778, Clinton sent 3,500 men under Lieutenant-Colonel Archibald Campbell down to attack the busy port city of Savannah, Georgia. General Augustine Prevost came up from Florida to join him. At first the Rebels, under General Robert Howe, tried to beat off the attack. Then an old Negro led Campbell's men through the wooded swamps until they were behind Howe. Assaulted on both sides, the Americans panicked and fled—many were drowned in the swamps. The American losses were eighty-three dead, 453 captured. Three British were killed and ten wounded. After this capture of Savannah, the British ruled Georgia again.

The following September, the French fleet under Admiral d'Estaing appeared off the Georgia coast. The combined American and French forces were 5,000 against 3,200 British. On October 4, 1779, French and American batteries began shelling Savannah. The bombardment was so fierce that of 450 homes there was hardly one that "had not been shot through." But d'Estaing was afraid of what autumn storms could do to his fleet. In spite of protests, he insisted on a head-on dawn attack on Savannah. It was a disaster. It was the battle of Bunker Hill the other way round, with the French and Americans taking the losses. The allies lost more than 800, the British only 150.

D'Estaing refused to carry on the siege and sailed away. Another attempt at a joint American land and French sea action had failed, leaving the Americans very bitter.

The Americans' failure to capture Savannah was followed in the spring by a greater Rebel disaster—General Benjamin Lincoln's loss of the city of Charleston.

Sir Henry Clinton attacked Charleston by land, with an army far larger than that defending it. The city was soon surrounded. The one escape route was cut off by two British officers, Lieutenant-Colonel Banastre Tarleton and Major Patrick Ferguson, with their Tory regiments. The siege lasted a month. Each day the British moved nearer the city. On May 9, 1780, the British offered peace terms. The Americans answered with a bombardment. "Shells like meteors crossed each other, cannon balls whizzing, shells hissing, ammunition chests blowing up."

After this last defiance, as the American Colonel William Moultrie wrote later in his memoirs, we "began to cool, and we cooled gradually, and on the 11 May we capitulated and on the morning of the twelfth we marched out."

A British officer described the surrender of Charleston thus: "The General limped out at the head of the most ragged rabble I ever beheld. . . . They laid down their arms. . . . The militia began to creep out of their holes the next day." The British took 5,000 prisoners and masses of supplies. It was the greatest American disaster of the war.

Colonel Moultrie also recalled that an English captain said to him, "Sir, you have made a gallant defense, but you have a great many rascals among you who came out every night and gave us information of what was passing in your garrison."

Not only was Charleston lost but 350 Virginians who had been marching to its rescue were attacked by Tarleton near Waxhaws Creek, in South Carolina. Tarleton claimed afterwards that the Rebels seemed about to fire on his white flag of truce. In any case, he permitted his soldiers to massacre every surrendering American. It was "a bloody day, that wanted only the war-dance and roasting-fire to have it placed first in the records of torture and death in the West." The massacre of Waxhaws inspired the Rebel war-cry "Tarleton's Quarter! Tarleton's Quarter!" and was used as an excuse for much future Rebel cruelty.

South Carolina and Georgia were in British hands. Clinton, satisfied, returned to New York City, leaving Lord Cornwallis to carry on the campaign to subdue the south with 8,000 soldiers. Cornwallis set up bases along the coast at Savannah, Georgia, Beaufort and Charleston, South Carolina and Georgetown, Virginia.

But American guerrillas undercut Cornwallis's communications, struck at his outposts and attacked his Tories. The Revolution in the south became a bitter civil war—much of its cruelty caused by revenge for the massacre at Waxhaws. Families were torn apart. Friends and neighbors became savage enemies and the whole country sprang into "an absolute state of rebellion."

Congress, without consulting Washington, named Horatio Gates General in the south. Stupidly, he began a march through wilderness swampland swarming with Tories. Although his men were sick, tired and hungry, on August 15, he ordered a night march, boasting: "I will breakfast tomorrow with Lord Cornwallis at my table"—as a prisoner, of course.

Cornwallis had ordered a night march too. The two armies were startled to meet halfway, in a pine forest, at about two in the morning. Cornwallis arranged his battle line carefully to await the dawn. Gates, just as the fight was starting, suddenly tried to shift his exhausted, untrained militia. Confusion resulted. The British Light Infantry took advantage of it and charged. Only a handful of regular Rebel soldiers stood their ground. Cornwallis, seeing that no cavalry opposed him, pushed his dragoons on and his infantry smashed ahead with fixed bayonets. The Rebel militia threw down their arms and ran.

General Gates, on an excellent horse, ran faster than anyone else. He did not stop running until he reached Charlotte, North Carolina, sixty miles from the battle. A month later a sarcastic advertisement appeared in a New York City newspaper. It began:

REWARD

Strayed, lost or stolen . . . on the 17 August last, near Camden, in the State of South Carolina, a whole ARMY consisting of horse, foot and dragoons, to the amount of near TEN THOUSAND. . . .

Alexander Hamilton, George Washington's secretary (later to be the first American Secretary of the Treasury), wrote even more scornfully of Gates's cowardice, "Was there ever an instance of a general running away as Gates has done from his whole army? . . . One hundred and eighty miles in three days and a half. It does admirable credit to the activity of a man at his time of life. But it disgraces the general and the soldier."

Colonel Banastre Tarleton

47

Hunger and Treachery

*T*he war in the northern states seemed to stand still. Two winters and a summer passed without any great battle.

In the spring of 1779 Sir Henry Clinton received orders from London: "Bring Mr. Washington to a decisive and general action" (that is, beat him in one big battle). But Clinton found it hard to do this, for Washington was determined not to risk his whole army in one battle unless he could be sure of winning it. So, although leaders in Congress kept clamoring for something to happen, he hung on, waiting for the right moment.

In the meantime, Clinton captured several forts on the Hudson River, one of them at Stony Point. On July 15, Washington sent "Mad Anthony Wayne" with a picked band of men in a silent midnight bayonet attack, to re-take Stony Point. (Wayne got his nickname because he was so reckless.) His soldiers fought, as Wayne wrote to Washington, "like men determined to be free," and the fort was again in American hands.

After this little happened. The two enemies watched each other keenly, but neither would risk a battle. So the summer passed and in October Clinton moved his troops down to New York for the winter.

On December 1, 1779, Washington rode into winter quarters in Morristown, New Jersey. The winter of 1779–80 was one of "dreadful extremity." There were blizzards, thick ice, screaming winds, destitution and hunger, bitter grumblings among the soldiers, and even mutiny. The French furnished uniforms for the American Army, but other supplies were lacking. There were so many shortages that Washington wrote: "Our affairs are in a more distressed, ruinous and deplorable state than they have been since the commencement of the war."

One soldier wrote that all he had eaten in four days was a little black birch bark "which I knaw off" a stick of wood. He saw men roasting their old shoes and eating them!

The snow was still eight inches deep at the end of March. It was a summer of suffering, too. The thirteen states still held their purse strings "as though they would damn the world rather than part with a dollar to their army." Washington's troops shrank from 25,000 to 3,000 men. There was so little food that he had to turn militia away.

At one moment Washington was hopeful, for a French fleet arrived. Disappointment again! A larger British fleet prevented the French from attacking. Then the bad news of General Gates's defeat arrived. Finally, came one of the bitterest shocks of all. Major-General Benedict Arnold, the hero of Quebec, Ticonderoga and Saratoga, had turned traitor! This is how General Nathanael Greene's Orders of the Day for September 26, 1780 described Arnold's treachery:

"Treason of the blackest dye was yesterday discovered. General Arnold who commanded at West Point, lost to every sentiment of honour and of public and private obligation, was about to deliver up that important fort into the hands of the enemy . . . Arnold, the traitor, made his escape to the enemy. Mr André, Adjutant-General of the British Army, who came out as a spy to negotiate the business is our prisoner."

Benedict Arnold was a brave soldier, but he had been

Mrs. Benedict Arnold

made bitter by the promotion of younger officers over his head. He was a man who liked to spend money, and he had a young and extravagant bride. When he was military governor of Philadelphia, in 1778, he had been dishonest about public property and made money for himself. Congress had questioned his actions and he was court-martialed in the winter of 1780.

While the court-martial was pending, Arnold decided, for money, to go over to the British side. He approached Sir Henry Clinton secretly. Arnold's go-between was a china-dealer in Philadelphia who put him in touch with Clinton's adjutant and intelligence officer, Major John André. André and Arnold wrote to each other in code. Arnold sent André military information to pass on to Clinton.

Papers still exist, written by André, that give his ideas on how Arnold could help the British. Clinton himself suggested that Arnold should accept a command, "be surprised and cut off. . . . A service of this nature involving five or six thousand men would be rewarded with twice as many thousand guineas," Clinton promised. The court-martial found Arnold guilty on four of eight counts, and sentenced him to a formal rebuke from Washington. Arnold grew more bitter. He begged Washington to give him command of West Point, the important fortress on the Hudson River. Washington, because of Arnold's brave record, agreed. On July 15, 1780, Arnold wrote Clinton a letter in code offering to sell West Point to the British for £20,000. When, on August 3, Arnold took command of West Point, his dreams of profitable treason seemed about to be fulfilled.

Arnold arranged for André to come up the Hudson to a secret meeting. There they would make final arrangements for the betrayal. The two men met on the riverbank at midnight on September 21. Arnold gave André papers to take back to Clinton. They included a map of West Point, information on the fort's armaments, summaries of Washington's secret orders—some of them in Arnold's own writing. André hid these papers in his shoes under his stockings.

Arnold was afraid that spy boats on the river might stop André if he tried to return to British lines by the Hudson. André was persuaded to change from his uniform to a claret-colored coat with gold trim. (Clinton had warned André to keep on his British uniform. Then if he were caught he would be treated as a prisoner of war, not a spy.) André was also persuaded to return by land, and was given a pass, which Arnold himself signed. André reluctantly took this fatal advice both in the matter of clothes, and in the means of going back to New York.

On his way back to safety, André was stopped by three Rebel militiamen. In searching him for money, they found the papers in his shoes. André was taken to the commander of a nearby dragoon detachment. His papers were sent on to Washington. By mistake they first reached Arnold, who was eating his breakfast. After warning his wife, Arnold fled to the *Vulture,* a British warship moored in the Hudson.

Pretty Mrs Arnold's wails and tears convinced Washington's young officers that she must be innocent (although she was probably deeply involved in the plot). She also convinced Washington, and was allowed to join her husband in New York.

*Major General
Benedict Arnold*

André was tried and sentenced to hang as a spy. Charles Stedman, the Loyalist historian, said, "the board of officers fixing their attention upon the naked fact of his being in disguise within their lines . . . were of the opinion that he came under the description and ought to suffer the punishment of a spy."

André's courage and dignity impressed his American captors deeply. When "he met his fate like a brave man" there was as much grief in the American camp as in British headquarters. Major André's body now lies in Westminster Abbey, where it was taken after the Revolution.

Arnold reached New York City in safety. He was given over £6,000 and a pension for his wife, and was named a brigadier-general, but, as you can imagine, he was very unpopular in the British Army.

West Point was safe. The link between the New England and Middle states was safe. Arnold's treason had failed, but it shocked the men who had trusted him so long. One of his officers wrote: "Treason, treason! treason! black as h-ll! . . . We were all astonishment, each peeping at his next neighbor to see if any treason was hanging about him."

A Land Laid Waste

*T*reachery in the north. Defeat in the south—by October 1780 the Rebel cause had touched its darkest depths. The government was weak. After six years of war the citizens seemed ready to let their army starve. Money had gone down in value, until Washington said it took a wagon-load of money to buy a wagon-load of food.

Then on October 7, 1780, at King's Mountain upon a high ridge between South and North Carolina, the Rebels won a battle! Every man on both sides of the battle, except the British commander, Major Patrick Ferguson, was a colonial—Rebel or Loyalist. It was the only battle of the Revolution entirely between Americans.

"Bull Dog" Ferguson was the best rifleman in the British Army. His raids were feared as much as Banastre Tarleton's, so when Cornwallis sent him into the North Carolina back-country, to organize the Tories there, the Rebel frontiersmen gathered 3,000 strong to drive him out. They pursued him and his 1,000 Tories to high, stony King's Mountain.

Ferguson waited on top of the ridge. The Rebels dismounted, tied up their horses, and pushed, in a light rain, in horseshoe formation, through the sheltering trees. Shooting and reloading, they fought from tree to tree to the summit. Ferguson, vowing he would "never yield to such damned bandits," rushed forward, hacking with his sword until he was shot down. Immediately, his men surrendered.

With the vengeful shout, "Tarleton's Quarter! Tarleton's Quarter!" the Rebels killed many of the surrendering Loyalists. The Battle of King's Mountain lasted only an hour.

On the same day as King's Mountain, Congress, finally heeding Washington's wishes, replaced General Gates by General Greene. When Greene, with von Steuben to train his raw troops, reached Charlotte, North Carolina, in December 1780, he found only 1,500 men fit for duty. (Having won at King's Mountain, the militia as usual all went home.) Greene also found he had only enough food for three days, and no money. His army "was wretched beyond description," Greene wrote, "so addicted to plundering they were a terror to the inhabitants." He added also, "Whigs and Tories pursue each other with little less than savage fury."

Since Cornwallis had three men to his two, and the countryside had been laid waste, Greene decided guerrilla warfare, was his only hope. He sent out Daniel Morgan, the buckskinned giant whose riflemen had shot so well at Saratoga. Morgan met Banastre Tarleton with 750 men at Cowpens in South Carolina. It was a bitterly cold morning, January 17, 1781. Tarleton ordered an immediate attack. The first two Rebel lines fell back before Tarleton's onrush. Then, in from either side, Morgan's men closed in a bayonet charge. Tarleton lost hundreds in dead, wounded and prisoners. Twelve Rebels were killed, sixty wounded. The Battle of Cowpens, Cornwallis said, "almost broke my heart."

Cornwallis was determined to avenge Cowpens. So he set out after the Rebels as fast as he could go. Morgan was too weak to risk another battle. In a 100-mile two-day march, he joined Greene. Cornwallis was so keen to catch Morgan and Greene that he burned most of his supplies, baggage and wagons because they were slowing him up. He burned things he would afterwards need desperately. To set an example, he even burned his personal belongings.

Greene led Cornwallis on a "country dance," through icy, muddy roads north toward Virginia, then back into North Carolina, into West Virginia and finally back into North Carolina. What was left of the British supplies was long since finished by then.

Then on March 15, 1781 (before his militia got restless and went home "to kiss their wives and sweethearts") Greene picked a battleground and waited for Cornwallis's attack. He chose a place near thickly wooded ground. Since a brick courthouse stood on a nearby hill, the fight was known as the Battle of Guilford Courthouse.

Greene had 4,500 men against Cornwallis's 1,900. Greene arranged his lines as Morgan had at Cowpens. He put his raw troops in the front, telling the men behind them "to shoot down the first man that runs." But—alas—once the front row had fired its volleys, it fled. The "long, obstinate and bloody" battle was after all won by superior British artillery. But one out of every four of Cornwallis's men fell. Charles James Fox, in London, said: "Another such victory would destroy the British Army."

Cornwallis's winning army was crippled. He had almost no supplies. He dared not stay inland any longer. He marched to the coast—to Wilmington—where the fleet could supply him with food and supplies. But he had no idea what Clinton wanted him to do. On April 10, 1781, Cornwallis wrote

General Greene

to Clinton: "I am very anxious to receive Your Excellency's commands, being totally in the dark as to the intended operations of the summer."

He then wrote to another general: "I am quite tired of marching about the country in quest of adventures."

If Cornwallis was in the dark about what his commander expected of him, Greene was not. Doggedly he started to destroy the British posts in the interior. In this he was aided by Francis Marion and his guerrillas. Marion had become an almost legendary person. He could strike at Tory forces without warning and get away without being caught. Banastre Tarleton named him "The Swamp Fox," and so he is known in American history. Sometimes he had less than twenty men in his band, sometimes several hundred. Greene used Marion and his men with great success.

Not that Greene was winning battles in the summer of 1781. In fact he lost three battles. Like Washington he lost his battles and won his campaigns. With Marion the Swamp Fox to help him, he could write to the French envoy, "We fight, get beat, rise and fight again."

It must never be forgotten that more than 5,000 Negroes fought for American independence. First and most famous was Crispus Attucks, shot down in the Boston Massacre. There were Negro Minute Men as well as white ones at Lexington, Concord and Bunker Hill. One of the bravest was a freedman, Peter Salem.

When Washington took command of the Rebel army, Negroes were forbidden to join. But later, after the English offered freedom to any slave who enlisted in the British army, Congress lifted the ban. The Rebels desperately needed the help of every able-bodied man. Negroes took part in major battles such as Saratoga, Monmouth and Yorktown.

There were Negroes in the little American navy. One, a captain from Virginia, Mark Starlin, was reclaimed by his master when the Revolution ended. He died in slavery! Negroes were also effective as spies. A slave, Pompey, helped win the Battle of Stony Point by bringing Mad Anthony Wayne the British password. Another, James Armistead, was a double spy. He took false information to Cornwallis, and carried back the truth to Lafayette.

More than 100,000 slaves were freed as a direct result of the Revolution. More than 100,000 "voted with their feet" and left the United States for Canada, the West Indies and England after the war. In spite of the part they played, more than 80 years were to pass between the end of the American Revolution and the end of Negro slavery in America.

Lord Cornwallis

The World Turned Upside Down

*T*he British generals never seemed able to work together. First it was Burgoyne and Howe who disagreed; now it was Clinton and Cornwallis. Cornwallis believed that winning in Virginia could mean winning the entire war. He wanted Clinton to leave New York and gather the whole British army together in Virginia. Clinton had 20,000 men idling in New York. But he dared not leave the city, for Washington would pounce in and take it. So the two British commanders disagreed. In May 1781, Cornwallis moved into Virginia and took command of the 7,000 British troops there. After some time he received direct orders from Clinton to move to the coast, establish a base there, and send some of his army up to New York. So he marched down to Yorktown, a small port on the York River, off Chesapeake Bay.

Back in the north, a French land force under General Count Donatien de Rochambeau was working closely with Washington. Rochambeau "the ideal ally" had placed 4,000 French under Washington's command. He also gave Washington $20,000 from his war chest. But without naval help, Rochambeau and Washington could do nothing against Clinton's 17,000 men in New York.

Then in August 1781, Rochambeau heard from Admiral François Joseph de Grasse. De Grasse planned to come from the West Indies to Chesapeake Bay later in the month. His orders allowed him to stay only until the middle of October. Then he must return to the West Indies to defend the French islands there. Here was Washington's hoped-for chance! If he could get his whole army down to Virginia to attack Yorktown from the land, and de Grasse could attack it from the sea, Cornwallis's army could be destroyed.

A short time before, a letter from Washington to Lafayette inviting him to come north and join in an attack on New York had fallen into British hands. This convinced the British that the Rebels' main aim was to capture New York. Washington had now completely changed his plan, but it was easy to deceive Clinton into thinking that he was still going to attack the city. In fact, he planned a rapid, secret march to Virginia, leaving only 2,000 men behind to hoodwink Clinton in New York. He did not even tell his own men where they were going.

On August 15, 1781, Washington alerted his army of Americans and French: "General Orders are now issued for the army to prepare for movement at a moment's notice." By August 20, they were on their way—where to? To New York, they thought, but at Kingsbridge they were ordered to "right about." As they marched, the soldiers betted on where they were off to. Most still thought they were making for the New Jersey shore of the Hudson River to aid in a siege of New York. At last, on the twenty-first, they knew! "We are stealing a march on the enemy," one of them wrote, "and are actually destined for Virginia in pursuit of the army under Lord Cornwallis!"

Americans and French marched through Paramus, Springfield and Princeton. Wagons carried their packs so that they could march faster. The army buzzed with rumors—was it true that a French fleet was on its way to help? They crossed Pennsylvania. Marching through Philadelphia their two-mile-long line raised "dust like a smothering snow." Then they marched through Maryland till they reached the point where boats were ready to carry them down the Chesapeake and up the James River to Williamsburg in Virginia. (Washington was able to go home to Mount Vernon, his great plantation in Virginia, for the first time since 1776.) Lafayette, who was watching outside Yorktown, kept getting messages from Washington, telling of troops, heavy cannon and ammunition on the way, and asking, "But what has become of de Grasse and the French fleet?"

De Grasse and his fleet were on their way too. He was racing the British admirals Graves and Hood to the Chesapeake. He got there first. French ships blocked the James River, preventing Cornwallis from crossing and escaping to the south. French ships sealed off the York River. French ships guarded the mouth of the Chesapeake.

Then the French and British fleets met in battle on September 5, 1781. There were twenty-four ships from France, to nineteen British ships. Graves blundered and, before he could correct his error, another French fleet had come up to reinforce de Grasse.

Saying "We cannot succor him nor venture to keep the sea any longer," Graves sailed away, leaving Cornwallis without any help from the British navy.

When the French and Americans arrived outside of Yorktown, between September 14 and 24, they made a semicircle

The Marquis de Lafayette

around Cornwallis's strongly built defenses. The Americans were on the right, the French on the left. The French fleet controlled the bay.

Rebel militia poured into camp as they had poured in at Boston, at Saratoga, King's Mountain and Cowpens. When on October 9, Washington touched off the first cannon, 16,000 French and Americans hemmed in Cornwallis's 6,000.

Across the river on the Gloucester shore, Armand Louis, Duc de Lauzun (one of the French allies), kept Banastre Tarleton in check.

Washington had one final great worry—would de Grasse stay long enough to complete the siege, long enough to force Yorktown to surrender? On September 23, a letter came from de Grasse. It told Washington that the French had to leave for the West Indies by October 16.

Washington wrote back urgently: "The enterprise against Yorktown under the protection of your ships is as certain as any military operation can be . . . and its consequences must necessarily go a great way towards terminating the war."

Washington sent Rochambeau and Lafayette to plead his case. They got de Grasse's promise. He would stay after October 15, if need be. (Cornwallis started surrender negotiations on the seventeenth.)

From October 10 to 15, there was a "tremendous incessant firing from the American and French batteries . . . the British ships were wrapped in a torrent of fire . . . the bomb-shells from the besiegers and besieged incessantly crossing each other."

On October 16, at eleven o'clock at night, Lord Cornwallis made one last try to break out of the trap. He sent the first of three groups of men across the York River at Gloucester Point where the American line was weakest. They were to fight their way southward. But a sudden squall scattered the boats. When at two o'clock in the morning the storm was over, it was too late to bring the rest of the men across. As Tarleton wrote, "soon after daybreak they returned under the fire of the enemy's batteries to Earl Cornwallis at Yorktown. . . . Thus expired the last hope of the British Army."

Cornwallis's only chance of rescue was Clinton in New York. But Clinton either could not or would not understand his extremity. Not until October 17, (the day surrender negotiations began) did he send troops from New York.

At ten o'clock on that same morning (the second anniversary of Burgoyne's surrender at Saratoga), through the powder and smoke, the Americans heard a beating drum. A little British drummer boy in scarlet had climbed on a parapet. He was beating for a parley. A big grenadier officer

French soldiers

climbed up beside him waving a white handkerchief. A young blue clad officer ran forward from the American lines.

Letters and flags of truce began traveling between Cornwallis's and Washington's headquarters. Before noon on October 19, "in the trenches before Yorktown" the surrender papers were signed. Washington and Rochambeau (de Grasse was ill) put their names to the terms Cornwallis had accepted.

Two o'clock of the same day was the formal surrender hour. The French soldiers in sparkling white, their weapons gleaming, marched to the west of the Hampton Road to Yorktown. The Americans in hunting shirt and buckskin, their worn uniforms of every color and kind, marched to the east.

General Charles O'Hara of the Guards rode out from the British lines. (Cornwallis, pleading illness, did not appear.) When O'Hara offered his sword to Washington, Washington said, "Never from such a good hand," but indicated that O'Hara, a second in command, should surrender to General Lincoln, the man who had suffered bitter defeat at Charleston.

As the British and Tories laid down their arms and were marched away, their bands played an old melody, *The World Turned Upside Down.* No one knew it at the time but the last great campaign, the last great battle for American independence, had been fought and won! And General Washington had won it. At the surrender of Yorktown his six-year-old dream came true. A joint French sea and American land force had decisively defeated the British army in America. As the poet, Lord Byron wrote of George Washington: "his was the all cloudless glory to free his country."

The Fate of the Loyalists

"*O*h, God, it is all over," Lord North cried when he heard about Cornwallis's surrender at Yorktown. But it was not all over! Two years passed before the Treaty of Paris ended the Revolution.

In those two years Washington held his hungry, unpaid, mutinous army together. Fighting in the United States dwindled to a few skirmishes in the south. In those two years England put all her strength into winning at sea. She won so well—against the French in the West Indies and the Spanish at Gibraltar—that by 1783 she could have set much stiffer terms than she did.

The Treaty of Paris, signed on September 3, 1783, gave the territory between the Allegheny Mountains and the Mississippi River to the United States. The Canadian–American boundary was much as it is now. Florida went to Spain.

Some very important questions had to be answered before the Treaty was signed. They concerned the Loyalists. What was to become of them? Must the Rebels give them back the property they had stolen? If the Rebels did not return the property, must they repay the Loyalists for their losses?

To the chief American negotiator, Benjamin Franklin, the Loyalists were America's "bitterest enemies." He warned England that if she wanted a peace treaty she had better "drop all mention of the refugees." By 1783 England wanted a peace treaty very much. She was sick of the American war. She wanted to end the American–French alliance. The English government also knew that, without fighting again, it could not force the Americans to repay the Loyalists for their losses.

Richard Oswald, an English negotiator, thought of a compromise which Congress accepted. He suggested that Congress should recommend that each state investigate the seizures of Loyalist property and, if they seemed unfair, to correct them.

Who were the Loyalists? What happened to them after the Revolution? The Loyalists (or as their enemies called them, the Tories) were Americans who after the Declaration of Independence in July 1776 wanted America to remain in the British Empire. Certain sorts of people were often Loyalists, such as government officials, lawyers, doctors, Anglican clergymen, large landowners in the north, small landowners in the southern states.

American legend had it that all Loyalists were rich and powerful, people who feared the Revolution would deprive them of their wealth and influence. Historians now know there were Loyalists among all groups, laborers and weavers as well as lawyers and landowners. Negro slaves became Loyalist when England promised them their freedom if they fought in the British army. Surprisingly, people who were not of English descent were more apt to be Loyalist than those whose ancestors had come from England.

Loyalist strength differed in each colony. They were strong in North Carolina, weak in South Carolina. Weakest in Massachusetts and Virginia, they were very strong in Pennsylvania and New York. If Loyalist New York and Pennsylvania had not been "put in awe" by strongly Rebel Massachusetts to the north, and Virginia to the south, they well might not have joined the Revolution at all! From the end of 1776 until after the Treaty of 1783 New York City remained in British hands. If the British had not yielded her up peacefully, it would have been almost impossible to get them out by force.

As in all civil wars the American Revolution broke up long friendships and loving families. The Rebel leader Benjamin Franklin never forgave his son William for remaining a Loyalist.

But nobody suffered more from the bitter feelings than the prisoners of war. At first the British did not treat their captives as prisoners of war, but as rebels and traitors. Only when many of their own men fell into American hands and they feared reprisals did they change their attitude and become somewhat less harsh.

The Rebels, by the same token, after the Declaration of Independence, considered the Loyalists traitors and criminals against the state, and treated them accordingly.

During the Revolution the Americans took about 15,000 prisoners, the British about 10,000. Neither side had the facilities to take care of their captives properly. Prisoners were packed into stinking jails made over from crowded warehouses, rotting ships and open mine shafts. They died from disease, filth, cold and hunger. Ill-treatment of prisoners, like the Indian raids, did much to increase American bitterness against the British and to harden feelings toward the Loyalists after the Revolution was over.

Loyalist recruiting poster

*Tory cartoon showing
how Rebels treated
Loyalists*

How many Loyalists were there? No one knows exactly, but there were Loyalists in every colony. Probably about one third of all the people who took an active part in the Revolution were Loyalist in sympathy.

Why, if there were Loyalists everywhere, and Great Britain's army and navy were behind them, did their side lose? The Loyalists never worked together as well as the Rebels did. They laughed at Sam Adams's Committees of Correspondence but never got together themselves so that Loyalists in one colony could exchange ideas and news, or even find out who were Loyalists in the other colonies.

Most important: before the Declaration of Independence many Loyalists and Rebels agreed politically on many things. They both resented the King's ministers. They both opposed taxation without representation. They both wanted a restoration of their Englishmen's rights. What they disagreed about was independence itself. The Loyalists feared the "mob rule" independence might bring far more than they resented Parliament's new taxes.

Since the two parties agreed on so much, the Loyalists were caught off guard when, in July 1776, independence was declared. Suddenly, after July 4, they were no longer considered law-abiding citizens, but traitors to their native land! And if their wealth and position made them the objects of envy, Rebel mobs threatened them with tar and feathers, and they fled out of the country.

Also, during the Revolution, some Loyalists seem to have been willing to let the British army do the fighting for them.

61

Admiral Howe's secretary once complained, "They all prate and profess much, but when you call upon them they do nothing."

On the other hand, when early in the war the Massachusetts Loyalists wanted to form their own regiments, the British army would not let them. But as the war dragged on and British losses mounted, Loyalist regiments were set up. Over 50,000 Loyalists fought. The names of some of their regiments were the British Legion, the King's Orange Rangers and the Maryland Loyalists.

What became of the Loyalists after the Revolution?

If their position did not excite envy in their neighbors, if they kept their political opinions to themselves, if they never fought against the Rebels, they could live quietly, without being attacked, right through the Revolution and afterwards. This was particularly true in New York, North Carolina and other states where there were Loyalist communities. Many of them continued to live much as they had before the Revolution started, and became leaders in the young American republic. But if they left the country during the Revolution or joined the British army, their lands and property were confiscated.

Early in the Revolution, 1,000 Massachusetts Loyalists sailed with Howe from Boston to Halifax. Thousands more migrated later to Nova Scotia and Quebec. They created the province of New Brunswick. The descendants of the 60,000 exiles to Canada became very strong there. They did much to keep Canada in the British Empire and Commonwealth. Known as United Empire Loyalists, they have given Canada statesmen, warriors and educators.

Southern Loyalists traveled to the West Indies—where their heirs have preserved British traditions. The wealthiest Loyalists went to England. As early as 1775 they were dining together each week at the New England Club, meeting at the New England Coffee House on Threadneedle Street in London.

Though many Loyalists felt they had been betrayed, England generally treated them fairly and generously. By 1782 annual pensions totaling £70,000 were being awarded to them. After a Royal Commission was set up in 1783 to examine their claims, £3,000,000 more were distributed among them. In addition, £26,000 were given each year to Loyalists' widows and children. Settlers in Canada received almost £26,000,000.

After the Revolution some of the Loyalists prospered in England and on the Continent. Among these were the painters Gilbert Stuart and John Singleton Copley. (Copley's son became Lord Chancellor.) James Thompson from Massachusetts was a renowned scientist and inventor, an adviser to the King of Bavaria and a count of the Holy Roman Empire. (He took the title Count Rumford.)

But many of the 100,000 refugees grew homesick and some managed to go home again. Many more, however, stayed in exile, like all political refugees full of wrongs, dreams and stories of the old days. So numerous were they, one Loyalist wrote: "There will scarcely be a village in England without some American dust in it by the time we are all laid to rest."

Why were these Loyalists afraid to go home to America after the Revolution was over and the Peace Treaty signed? Why did a man like Washington call them "parricides" (father-murderers)? First, after the Declaration of Independence most Rebels automatically considered all Loyalists traitors to the United States. Second, during the war, Loyalists often had spied for the British army—on their Rebel friends and relatives. Worse, some Loyalists not only organized the brutal Indian raids along the frontiers, but put on war paint and led them. Also, the savage warfare in the southern states during the final years of the war (though the Loyalists were no crueller than the Rebels) left long and bitter memories behind.

These are some of the reasons why the Loyalists were resented by Rebels during their lives, and why, for generations afterward, they were condemned in American history and literature.

Few Englishmen—and certainly not George III—wanted to be tyrants or to oppress the colonies. In 1788, after it was all over, George III said about the Revolution: "We meant well to the Americans—just to punish them with a few bloody noses, and then make bows for the mutual happiness of the two countries. But want of principle got into the army, want of skill and energy in the First Lord of the Admiralty, and want of unanimity at home. We lost America."

Englishmen who valued their personal liberty eventually realized that the defeat at Yorktown had really done good because it had checked their country's "drift towards despotism." They came to see that the American colonies had not been lost in vain. As Horace Walpole put it: "Let us save the constitution. If England is free, and America is free, though disunited, the whole world will not be in vassalage." So, after the Revolution, while the new United States was making a new kind of government, England, under the leadership of William Pitt, Lord Chatham's son, became strong once more.

Count Rumford

Index

New Jersey and Pennsylvania

New York 1776

ROUTE OF BURGOYNE

ROUTE OF ST. LEGER

	3 Routes according to Burgoyne's Plan — destination Albany.— ■
××××××	Routes according to what really happened
A	Where St.Leger was halted.
B	Where Burgoyne surrendered at Saratoga.
C	Howe's route according to Burgoyne's Plan. He never came, but went instead to Philadelphia, Pa.

Burgoyne's plan and what happened

The War in the So